Lightning Bugs and Lullabies

written by Margaret Hillert
illustrated by Judy Hand

Library of Congress Catalog Card Number 87-91992
© 1988. The STANDARD PUBLISHING Company, Cincinnati, Ohio
Division of STANDEX INTERNATIONAL Corporation. Printed in U.S.A.

LIGHTNING BUGS

When God created lovely things,
He made some little stars with wings.
I watch the glimmer and the glow
As lightning bugs flash to and fro.

HOW DOES IT WORK?

I pet my kitten in the dark
And sometimes see a little spark.
At other times when it is night,
Behind her eyes she lights a light.
And way down underneath her fur
I feel a rumbly kind of purr.
A motor runs inside her skin.
I think God must have plugged it in.

SMALL CREATURES

Some of God's small creatures
Hide themselves the whole day through
And only come out after dark
To do the things they do.

THE ANSWER

"Who? Who are you?"
The hoot owl calls
From somewhere in the wild.
"Who? Who are you?"

I know. I know.
I am God's perfect child.

LULLABY

Sleep, little teddy bear.
Close up your eyes.
Sleep while the baby moon
Sleeps in the skies.
Teddy bears need a rest.
Really they do.
And while you're sleeping,
I'll take a nap, too.

NIGHT LIGHT

My night light is a little cross
That shines against the wall.
It doesn't give a lot of light
Because it is so small,
But it reminds me all night long
God's love for me is big and strong.

ENCHANTED SKY

Rose over silver
And silver over blue.
Golden fountains splashed with green,
And darkness showing through.
Bits of colored stardust
That drift and slowly fade.
What a brief enchanted sky
The fireworks have made!
But when the show has ended
For yet another year,
God's stars just keep on shining.
They never disappear.

NIGHT AND DAY

When I am in my bed at night
I see a corner of the sky
Where God has set the stars alight
And hung the moon like some bright eye
That watches me while I'm asleep.

When I awake the sun is there,
And bird song fills the morning air.
I throw my covers in a heap.
And then, to start the day just right,
I talk awhile to God in prayer.

THE LIGHTHOUSE

The lighthouse standing out to sea
Sends forth a steady beam of light
That warns the ships away from harm
And guides them safely through the night.
And Jesus lights a path for me
To keep me safe and guide me right.

NIGHT SHADOWS

When I'm outside, I run and play.
Our maple never moves all day.
But when night comes, it's strange to see
That somehow it has followed me.
I find its shadow on my wall,
Trunk and branches, leaves and all.
And somewhere in its shadows deep
There might be shadow birds asleep.
And soon I shall be sleeping, too,
While God keeps watch the whole night through.

NIGHT SNOW

Whitely, lightly, brightly,
Softly without sound,
Whirling, twirling, curling
Like feathers to the ground,
Blowing, glowing, growing
Higher flake by flake,
Piling up God's treasure
For the morning when I wake.

LULLABY

Hushaby, rockaby.
Sleep, little baby.
Hushaby, rockaby.
Sleep, little dear.
Hushaby, rockaby.
Mother is holding you,
Daddy is watching,
And Jesus is near.

STORY TIME

When I have settled in my bed
And have my favorite toy,
My daddy tells me stories
Of when Jesus was a boy.
And there's David and Goliath,
And how Noah built the ark.
I like the Bible stories
Daddy tells when it gets dark.

BEDTIME PRAYER

I'm not afraid to go to bed.
I never cover up my head.
I know that You are everywhere
And I am always in Your care.
But, Lord, I hope that You will keep
The stars all lighted while I sleep.